In memory of my parents, Darrell and Bonnie Sanders,
whose love was undeniable and never denied
—RS

To all the LGBTQ+ identifying people who have fought,
and those who still fight, for the rights we have today,
thank you
—RC

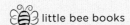 little bee books

New York, NY
Text copyright © 2021 by Rob Sanders
Illustrations copyright © 2021 by Robbie Cathro
All rights reserved, including the right of reproduction
in whole or in part in any form.
All photographs used with permission from Jack Baker and Michael McConnell.
Additional credits: Paul Hagen, photo of Jack and Michael with their wedding
rings, and photo of Jack and Michael with their wedding cake; Angela Jimenez,
photo of Jack and Michael after the SCOTUS Marriage Equality Decision; Melissa
Davidson, photo of Jack and Michael circa 2016
For information about special discounts on bulk purchases,
please contact Little Bee Books at sales@littlebeebooks.com.
Manufactured in China RRD 0121
First Edition
2 4 6 8 10 9 7 5 3 1
ISBN 978-1-4998-0956-5

glaad.org
littlebeebooks.com

A PROUD PARTNERSHIP BETWEEN

glaad + little bee books

A portion of the proceeds from the sale of this
book will be donated to accelerating
LGBTQ acceptance.

TWO GROOMS on a CAKE

The Story of America's First Gay Wedding

by Rob Sanders   illustrated by Robbie Cathro

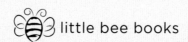 little bee books

Two grooms on top of a cake.

That's us.

Some thought it could never happen.

And it almost didn't.

But one day, we stood in frosting
on top of a three-tiered wedding cake.

This is our story.

Every cake begins with a recipe.

Ours did, too.

The recipe told exactly
what was needed, down to
the smallest pinch.

And it gave instructions
for every single step.

There are no recipes for weddings.
But there are laws for marriages.

In 1971, two men who loved each other
weren't allowed to marry.

Neither were two women in love.

That meant we weren't allowed
to stand together on a cake.

At least, not yet.

Of course, a cake needs ingredients.

Our recipe called for fresh eggs, creamy butter,
and the sweetest of sugar.

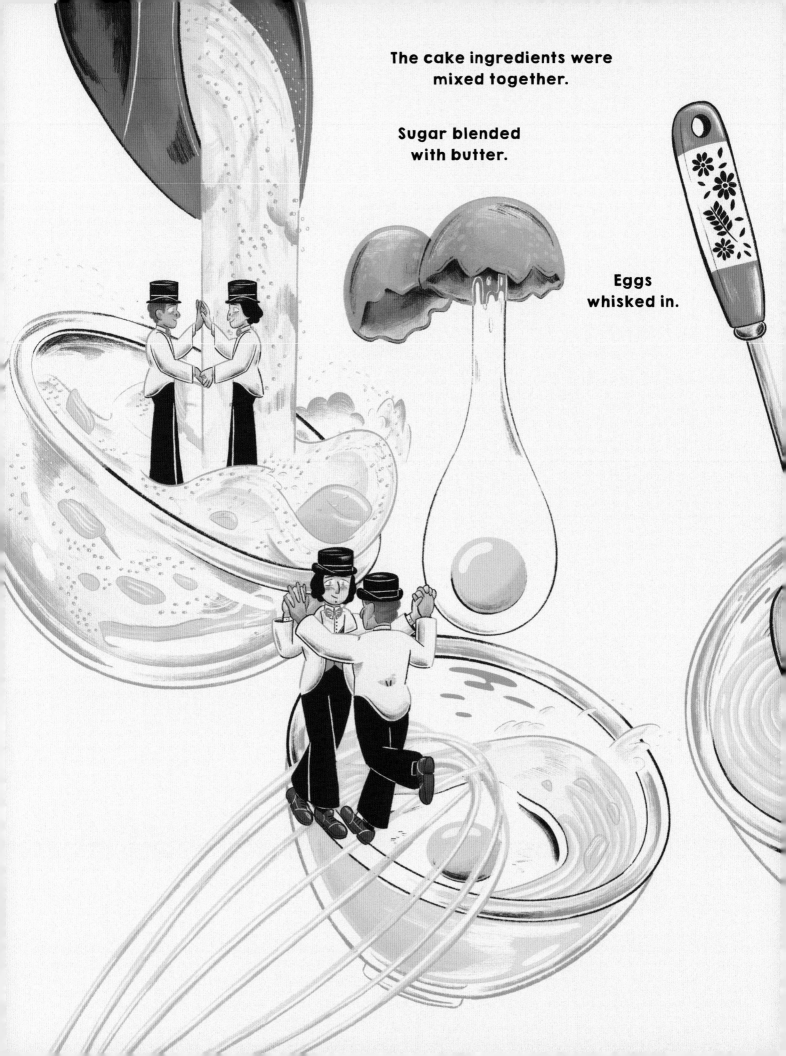

The cake ingredients were mixed together.

Sugar blended with butter.

Eggs whisked in.

Flour folded into
the batter.

One item introduced at a time until
all the ingredients knew each other.

Until the ingredients could
work well together.

Jack and Michael had to get to know each other, too.

They dated.

They spent
time together.

They learned more
about each other.

Once the ingredients were combined,
one last thing was added.

Love.

**Every baker knows
that's the secret to
the best cakes.**

**Then the batter was
poured into pans.**

**The pans were slid into
a steaming oven.**

And we waited.

Baking takes time.

Love was added to Jack and Michael's relationship, too.

They decided to get married.

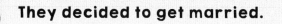

But it would take time to figure out
how two men could do that.

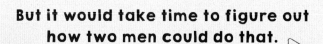

Jack found something in the law
that seemed to make it possible.

However, when the two men tried to get
a marriage license, they were told...

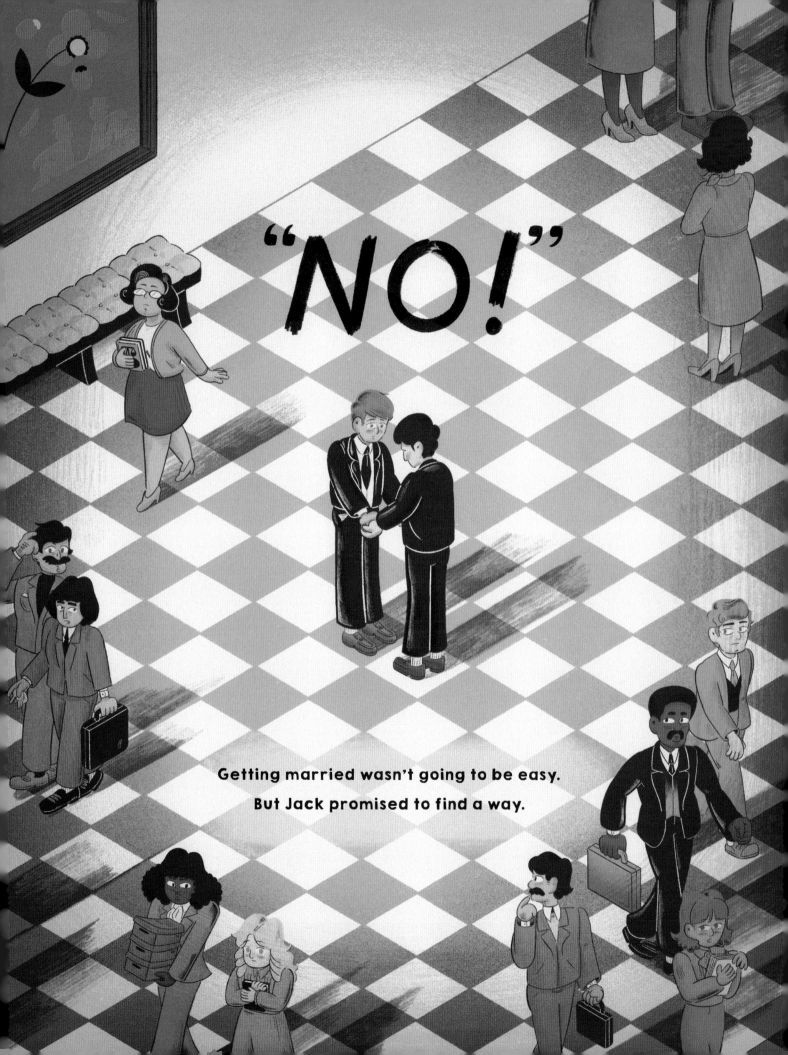

"NO!"

Getting married wasn't going to be easy.
But Jack promised to find a way.

Once our cake was baked, it had to cool.

We waited.

Trying to be patient.

Jack and Michael had to wait, too.
Their angry, hurt feelings needed time to cool off.

Jack studied the law, and
soon had a new idea.

What if no one realized the marriage
license was for two men?

Jack changed
his name to Pat.

Then Michael went alone
to the courthouse.

He applied for a second
marriage license.

The license was granted.

Our cake was nearly complete.

Each layer was covered
with thick, white frosting.

And the layers were stacked,
one . . . two . . . three tiers tall.

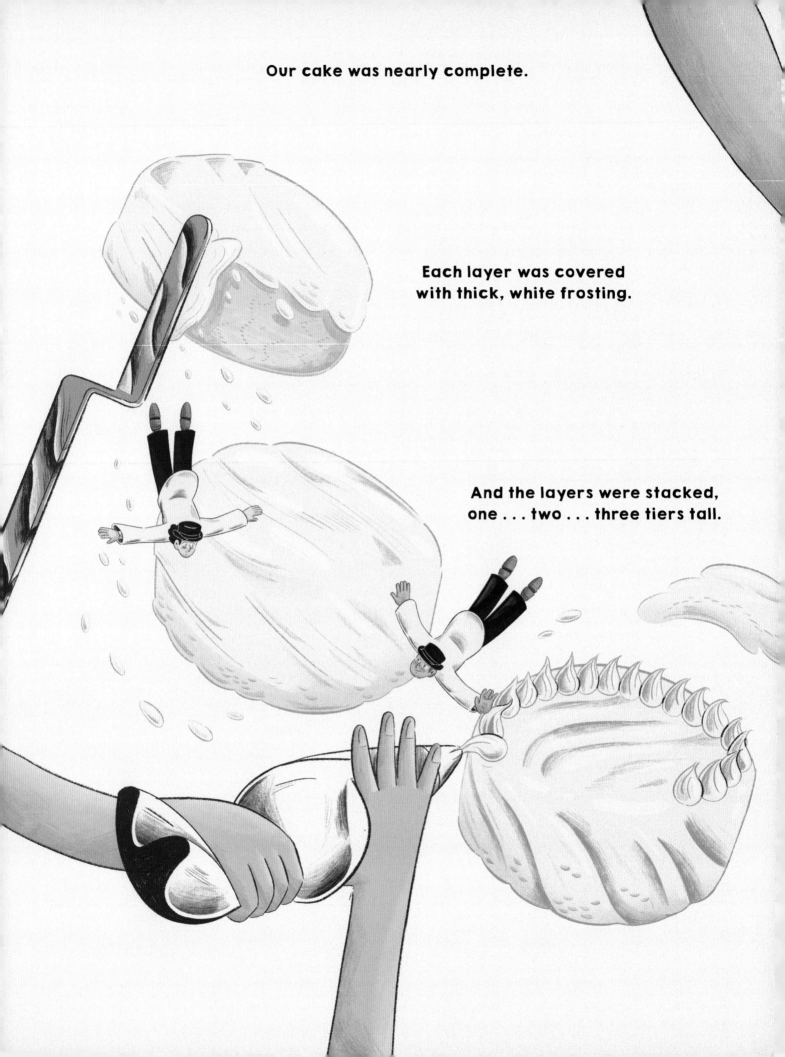

Then we were added.

Our feet planted firmly in the fluffy frosting.

We stood proudly side by side on top of the cake.

A wedding is not complete without the ceremony.

Jack and Michael set the date— *Friday, September 3, 1971.*

They sealed their marriage with a kiss.

"I do."
"I do."
"I will."
"I will."

It was the icing on the cake!

Michael and Jack smiled at us
as they cut the cake.

Friends snapped photos of
the two just-married grooms
and the two grooms on top of
the wedding cake.

Michael and Jack promised to
spend their lives together.

Years turned to decades.

Decades became a life together.

The two men grew deeper
and deeper in love.

Fifty years later, Jack and Michael
are still together.

Still married.

We know.

We've been with them all along.

Author's Note

Michael McConnell and Jack Baker met at a Halloween barn party in Norman, Oklahoma, on October 29, 1966. They soon started dating and on Jack's birthday, March 10, 1967, he asked Michael to be his lover. Michael replied, "Yes, but only if you agree to marry me legally." Marriage between two men was unheard of at the time, but Jack promised to find a way.

His promise led Jack to enroll in law school at the University of Minnesota in September 1969. Jack's careful study led to the discovery that the laws in Minnesota did not specifically say two men or two women could *not* marry. He learned in one of his first law courses about "equal protection under the law" and "what is not denied is permitted." He reasoned that since there was no specific law to prohibit gay marriage, it was therefore permitted.

Michael and Jack applied for a marriage license at the Hennepin County Courthouse on Michael's birthday, May 18, 1970. The license was quickly denied by the county. Michael and Jack sued, and years of court battles began. Their case became known as *Baker v. Nelson.*

Jack continued to study law and discovered that adoption would at least give him and Michael some legal protections, rights, and privileges similar to married couples. Michael adopted Jack, and Jack changed his name to the gender-neutral name of Pat Lyn McConnell. The name change gave the men another idea. They visited friends in a different county and lived with them until the legal waiting period of residents to wed was achieved. Michael went alone to the Blue Earth County Courthouse to apply again for a marriage license. This time the license was for Michael McConnell and Pat Lyn McConnell. The license was granted.

On Friday, September 3, 1971, at 9:15 p.m., Jack and Michael and a few of their friends gathered in a small apartment for the wedding. The Reverend Roger Lynn performed the ceremony. Friends stepped up to help. One designed and sewed wedding suits for Michael and Jack. Another made gold and silver wedding bands. Others designed wedding invitations and headbands for the couple, and one friend provided a cake, then took apart bride-and-groom cake toppers and placed the two grooms side by side on top of it.

After the wedding, the minister, Michael, Jack, and their witnesses signed the marriage certificate. That made it a legal marriage according to Minnesota law.

The case about Jack and Michael's first marriage license application eventually made its way all the way to the Supreme Court of the United States. On October 10, 1972, the justices dismissed the case with a one-sentence statement. But they did not entirely rule against Michael and Jack. In essence, the court said that the question about gay marriage was one that could not be answered at that time.

The clerk of Blue Earth County never officially recorded Jack and Michael's signed marriage certificate. But that didn't keep their marriage from being official. The license had been issued, witnessed, and certified. Blue Earth County and the state of Minnesota took no action against Jack and Michael's marriage, choosing instead to ignore the controversy.

Michael McConnell and Jack Baker remained the only legally married gay couple in the state of Minnesota for nearly forty-two years. On July 1, 2013, same-sex marriage became legal in that state, and marriage licenses began to be issued to same-sex couples that August. On June 26, 2015, the Supreme Court of the United States ruled in favor of marriage equality. In their decision, the justices decided it was finally time to rule on Jack and Michael's marriage application, which was originally denied by Hennepin County in 1970. They wrote, "*Baker v. Nelson* must be and is now overruled."

From that day on, marriage equality became the law of the land. On September 19, 2018, Minnesota Assistant Chief Judge Gregory Anderson found that Michael and Jack's wedding was legal "in all respects" and required Blue Earth County to officially record the marriage.

MARRIAGE EQUALITY TIMELINE

1970 ▸ Michael McConnell and Jack Baker apply for a marriage license. They are denied, and their case goes first to the state Supreme Court, then to the United States Supreme Court.

September 3, 1971 ▸ Michael McConnell and Jack Baker are married.

October 10, 1972 ▸ The United States Supreme Court dismisses Jack and Michael's case regarding their first marriage license.

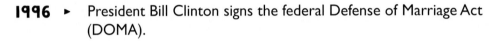

1973 ▸ Maryland becomes the first state to ban same-sex marriage.

1984 ▸ Berkeley, California, passes the nation's first domestic-partnership law.

1996 ▸ President Bill Clinton signs the federal Defense of Marriage Act (DOMA).

1997 ▸ Hawaii becomes the first state to offer domestic partnership benefits to same-sex couples.

1999 ▸ Vermont's Supreme Court rules that same-sex couples must receive the same benefits and protections as any other married couple under their state's constitution.

2000 ▸ The Central Conference of American Rabbis agrees to allow religious ceremonies for same-sex couples.
▸ Vermont becomes the first state to pass a law granting the full benefits of marriage to same-sex couples.

2003 ▸ California passes a domestic-partnership law which provides same-sex partners with almost all the rights and responsibilities as spouses in civil marriages.
▸ President Bush states that he wants marriage reserved only for heterosexual couples.
▸ The Massachusetts Supreme Court hands down a decision making it the first state to legalize gay marriage.

2004 ▸ The city of San Francisco begins marrying same-sex couples in an open challenge to California law.
▸ New Mexico begins issuing marriage licenses to same-sex couples since their marriage laws do not mention gender.
▸ Washington state agrees to permit same-sex marriage in a court decision.
▸ Several states pass initiatives to ban same-sex marriages.

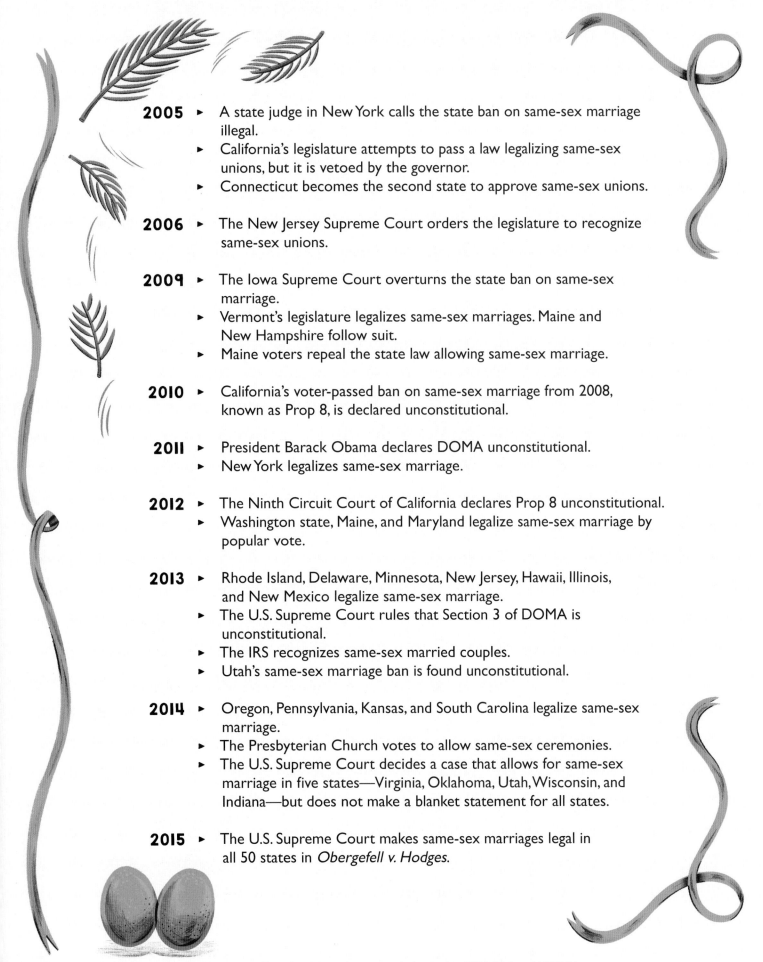

2005 ► A state judge in New York calls the state ban on same-sex marriage illegal.

► California's legislature attempts to pass a law legalizing same-sex unions, but it is vetoed by the governor.

► Connecticut becomes the second state to approve same-sex unions.

2006 ► The New Jersey Supreme Court orders the legislature to recognize same-sex unions.

2009 ► The Iowa Supreme Court overturns the state ban on same-sex marriage.

► Vermont's legislature legalizes same-sex marriages. Maine and New Hampshire follow suit.

► Maine voters repeal the state law allowing same-sex marriage.

2010 ► California's voter-passed ban on same-sex marriage from 2008, known as Prop 8, is declared unconstitutional.

2011 ► President Barack Obama declares DOMA unconstitutional.

► New York legalizes same-sex marriage.

2012 ► The Ninth Circuit Court of California declares Prop 8 unconstitutional.

► Washington state, Maine, and Maryland legalize same-sex marriage by popular vote.

2013 ► Rhode Island, Delaware, Minnesota, New Jersey, Hawaii, Illinois, and New Mexico legalize same-sex marriage.

► The U.S. Supreme Court rules that Section 3 of DOMA is unconstitutional.

► The IRS recognizes same-sex married couples.

► Utah's same-sex marriage ban is found unconstitutional.

2014 ► Oregon, Pennsylvania, Kansas, and South Carolina legalize same-sex marriage.

► The Presbyterian Church votes to allow same-sex ceremonies.

► The U.S. Supreme Court decides a case that allows for same-sex marriage in five states—Virginia, Oklahoma, Utah, Wisconsin, and Indiana—but does not make a blanket statement for all states.

2015 ► The U.S. Supreme Court makes same-sex marriages legal in all 50 states in *Obergefell v. Hodges*.

Source: http://guides.ll.georgetown.edu/c.php?g=592919&p=4182201

Michael, 1960

Jack, 1959

Our Wedding Day

With our cake

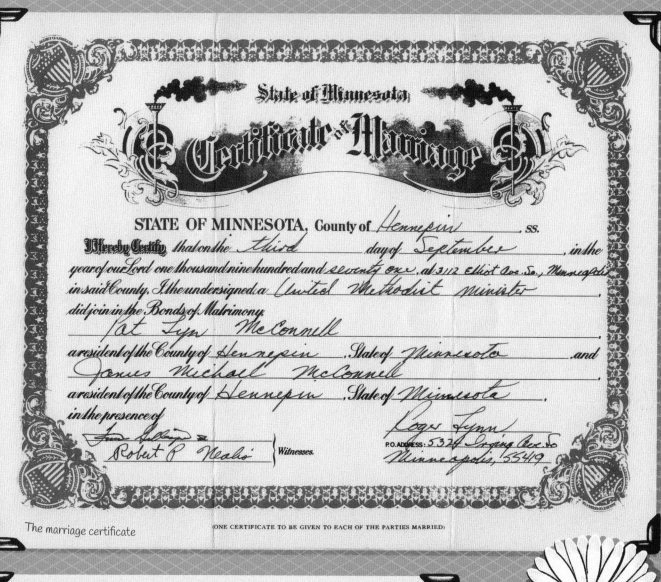

State of Minnesota
Certificate of Marriage

STATE OF MINNESOTA, County of *Hennepin* **ss.**

I Hereby Certify, that on the *third* *day of* *September* *, in the year of our Lord one thousand and nine hundred and* *seventy one* *, at 3112 Elliot Ave. So., Minneapolis in said County, I, the undersigned, a* *United Methodist* *minister, did join in the Bonds of Matrimony.*

Pat Lyn McConnell

a resident of the County of *Hennepin* *, State of* *Minnesota* *, and*

James Michael McConnell

a resident of the County of *Hennepin* *, State of* *Minnesota* *,*

in the presence of

Robert R. Neals } **Witnesses.**

Roger Lynn
P.O. ADDRESS: *5324 Irving Ave. So.*
Minneapolis, 55419

The marriage certificate

(ONE CERTIFICATE TO BE GIVEN TO EACH OF THE PARTIES MARRIED)

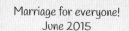

Marriage for everyone!
June 2015

Bibliography

Books

McConnell, Michael, Jack Baker, and Gail Langer Karwoski. *The Wedding Heard 'Round the World: America's First Gay Marriage.* Minneapolis: The University of Minnesota Press, 2016.

Pohlen, Jerome. *Gay & Lesbian History for Kids: The Century-Long Struggle for LGBT Rights.* Chicago: Chicago Review Press, 2015.

Sanders, Rob, and Jamey Christoph. *Stonewall: A Building. An Uprising. A Revolution.* New York: Random House, 2019.

Sanders, Rob, and Stephen Salerno. *Pride: The Story of Harvey Milk and the Rainbow Flag.* New York: Random House, 2018.

Sanders, Rob, and Jared Andrew Schorr. *Peaceful Fights for Equal Rights.* New York: Simon & Schuster Books for Young Readers, 2018.

Magazine Articles

"The Homosexual Couple," *Look: The American Family*, January 26, 1971, Volume 35, Number 2, pp. 69-71.

Jess Bravin, "Supreme Court Clerk Remembers First Same-Sex Marriage Case: Michel LaFond," *The Wall Street Journal*, May 1, 2015. Available online at: https://www.wsj.com/articles/supreme-court-clerk-remembers-first-same-sex-marriage-case-1430494015

Wedding Footage

First Gay Wedding in Minnesota—Jack Baker & Mike McConnell, 1971
https://www.youtube.com/watch?v=A1UYg8WoW9M

Interviews

Minnesota Couple Behind America's 1st Gay Marriage Shares Their Story
https://www.youtube.com/watch?v=ko2PNJZfX1Q

Interview: Minn. Couple Behind America's 1st Gay Marriage
https://www.youtube.com/watch?v=bzok4WpsBQs

A Celebration of the Michael McConnell Files
https://www.youtube.com/watch?v=ltwcoddfSrw

Pastor Reflects Back on Minn. Gay Marriage
https://www.youtube.com/watch?v=5MdGM9xBIMQ

Talks/Presentations

Telling Queer History with Michael McConnell
https://www.youtube.com/watch?v=gyliqlsfe4g

Michael McConnell Files/Archives
Jean-Nickolaus Tretter Collection in LGBT Studies, University of Minnesota Libraries

Personal Interviews and Correspondence

Notes from the author's ongoing conversations with Michael McConnell and Jack Baker